Body Work

poems

Stephanie Kaplan Cohen

 **Plain View Press**   http://plainviewpress.net
1101 W. 34th Street, STE 404   Austin, TX 78705

Copyright © 2018 Stephanie Kaplan Cohen. All rights reserved under International and Pan-American Copyright Conventions. No part of this book may be reproduced or distributed in any form or by any means, or stored in a data base or retrieval system, without written permission from the author. All rights, including electronic, are reserved by the author and publisher.

ISBN: 978-1-63210-033-7
Library of Congress Control Number: 2018933168

Cover art: *Abstract Face Woman Smiling*
© Madartists | Dreamstime.com
Madartists: https://www.dreamstime.com/madartists_info
Cover design by Pam Knight

Acknowledgments

Thanks to the following publications for prior publication of these poems:
"The Cross Dressing Cantaloupe" (*PMS: poemmemoirstory*, 2015); "Body Jumping" (*Westchester Review*, 2006); "My Mother Never Taught Me" (*Folly*, 2011); "Time Warp" (*Diverse Voices Quarterly*, 2015), "Yearly Visitation" (*Broken Plate*, 2016); "I Know Rivers" (*Spoon River Poetry Review*, 2016); "Misbegotten" (*riverSedge*, 2010); "The Morning Is Awash With Angels" (*Hawaii Pacific Review*, 2012); "I Am Moving Out of Grief Street" (*Willow Review*, 2015); "I'd Like To Kick the Glitter" (*Evening Street Review*, 2017); "Ladies and Gentlemen" (*Griffin*, 2016); "Never Mind the Mirror" (*Poet's Page*, 1999); "Life Is a Trade Off" (*Folly*, 2011); "A Proper Lady" (*Common Ground Review*, 2017); "Enough Already" (*Folly*, 2011); "Senior Marathon" (*Broad River Review*, 2017); and "God, Are You Angry?" (*riverSedge*, 2010).

We Find Healing In Existing Reality
Plain View Press is a 36-year-old issue-based literary publishing house. Our books result from artistic collaboration between writers, artists, and editors. Over the years we have become a far-flung community of humane and highly creative activists whose energies bring humanitarian enlightenment and hope to individuals and communities grappling with the major issues of our time—peace, justice, the environment, education and gender.

Dedicated to the memory

of my beloved husband

Charles Morris Cohen

*Thank you to Rebecca Shereff Martin
who had the vision and skill
to organize my stacks of poetry into this book.*

Contents

Body — 9
- Anatomy — 11
- Clitoris Talks to Umbilicus — 12
- A Gut Feeling — 13
- Haiku for Menopause — 14
- Heart and Soul — 15
- The Organ Players — 16
- Toilet Tissue Issues II — 17
- What Every Girl Wants — 18
- Weigh-In — 19
- The Cross Dressing Cantaloupe — 20

Family — 21
- A Bedtime Story From a Grandmother — 23
- Body Jumping — 24
- A Chair for My Mother — 25
- For Charles — 26
- Child of My Child — 27
- Forecast — 28
- Grandfather — 29
- Hits and Misses — 30
- I Used To Love — 31
- The Late Late Show — 32
- The Moon — 33
- Mother Love — 34
- My Father Taught Me — 35
- My Mother Never Taught Me — 36
- Of Late I Dream Correctively — 37
- Photography Lesson — 38
- Rachel at Almost Seven — 39
- Silence — 40
- A Telephone Call — 41
- Time Warp — 42
- Valentine's Day 2002 — 43
- Yearly Visitation — 44

Nature   45

    Bigoted Nature Lover   47
    Don't Say One Bad Word   48
    Every Autumn   49
    Hummingbird   50
    I Know Rivers   51
    Misbegotten   52
    The Morning Is Awash With Angels   53
    My Field of Flowers   54
    Procreation   55
    Sandy   56
    To Spring   57

Life   59

    The Chinese Summer   61
    The New Year   62
    Good Old Friend   63
    Failing Jewelry   64
    Feast of the Cafeteria   65
    I Am Moving Out of Grief Street   66
    I'd Like to Kick the Glitter   67
    Instructions for Any Room You Enter   68
    It's All a Matter of Taste   69
    Ladies and Gentlemen   70
    Look at Me   71
    Love, How the Hours Accumulate   72
    Mathematics Must Be True   73
    On a Perfect Sunday   74
    Terrible Things   75
    The Poem of Knowledge   76
    Vacuuming Heaven   77
    What Not   78
    When History Enters My House   79
    For Sale Signs   80
    Written in Stone   81

Age — 83

- Testing for Age — 85
- Never Mind the Mirror — 86
- Life Is a Trade Off — 87
- At Our Age — 88
- It's All Relative — 89
- A Proper Lady — 90
- Socks — 91
- Eighty-Year-Old Woman Attends Conference — 92
- Eighty Four — 93
- Enough Already — 94
- Fifty One Years and Still Counting — 95
- Hotsy Totsy — 96
- One Hundred Years From Now — 97
- Senior Marathon — 98
- Visibility Zero — 99
- The Old Woman in Two Shoes — 100
- What They Never Told You — 101
- What Time Is It — 102
- Scaladune — 103

Writing — 105

- Age Is Only a Number — 107
- Eagle — 108
- Sometimes a Poem Jumps Out at Me — 109
- Writing and Love and Love and Writing — 110
- Yes, We Have No Poems Today — 111

God — 113

- The Endless War — 115
- Everything Shall Be Known — 116
- God, Are You Angry? — 117
- God, Are You Really An Anti-Semite? — 118
- God Is Depressed — 119
- God Is Going Crazy — 120
- Feast on Your Life — 121

I'll Tell You a Secret	122
Law and Order	123
Looking at the Moon in Autumn	124
Six Thousand Body Bags	125
Count Me Out for the Recycle Bin	126
About the Author	127

Body

Anatomy

1. Corpuscles

Our doctor used to worry about the red ones
but nobody talks about them anymore.
My corpuscles are hurt by the inattention.
I have told them how much they mean to me
and how grateful I am for them soldiering on
despite their terrible snub.

2. Pancreas

Wherefore art thou, oh pancreas?
I know you to be somewhere near the liver,
doing whatever you do.
I am sure it is noble and mysterious work.
Not one medic has ever spoken of you.
Never mind, I love you anyway.

3. Anus

The hardest working part of the body
remains unmentionable,
gets rough treatment from scratchy tissue,
and no thanks for knowing
when to hold on or let go.
I propose a Thank You Anus Day.

Clitoris Talks to Umbilicus

Clitoris makes a comment,
addresses umbilicus.
I'm prettier than you,
a sweet nub, hidden, shy,
beautiful, responsive.

Umbilicus answers clitoris.
You cunt. You're there for fun.
I'm the lifesaver,
the giver of life.
You're just a piece of pleasure.

Without me, says clitoris,
without me, after you've done
your so-called job,
what is life worth
without some honest fun.

Nipple hangs down.
Shut up you two.
Look how nice
my other breast is.
We sit together in mutual admiration.

Clitoris and umbilicus
both blush, ashamed.
She needs us both.
Your knot is rather neat.
Your nub is a hidden treasure.

A Gut Feeling

Esophagus and intestines
are in trouble.
Esophagus whines,
Do you know how much she eats?
And I have to get it
all down to you.

I know, gut says,
I appreciate it,
and do you know
how I have to get
that mess down to stomach,
who says she's about to burst?

Colon chimes in:
Stommy sends down
half-eaten pieces
and so much
that I can't push it down,
no matter how hard I try.

Then someone sends down dynamite,
and excuse the expression,
but she shits so much
that poor rectum
is a bloody mess.

Esophagus yells, I've got it.
I won't let her swallow.
We'll all get a rest.
Gut does a little dance.
And colon sends out
a congratulatory fart.

Haiku for Menopause

The last time I bled
I blessed myself. There's still time.
Maybe just one more.

Heart and Soul

Heart says, I'm the one.
If I decide to stop,
for even a few minutes,
bam, you're all dead.

Brain speaks up.
You're such a hotshot,
pumping away. You're nothing
but a plumber.

Brain says, I control
thinking and action, and
I get to rest, which is
more than I can say for you.

Heart counters:
My indefatigable beat
is all you know, but
I send love.

And now,
come to think about it,
I even love you,
with your wise, quiet sense.

Brain blushes.
I'm sorry I called you a name,
and sends down
a warm deliciousness,

at which heart
gives a loud
thump
of thanks.

The Organ Players

Gall bladder and Liver
are duking it out.
I send the bile
that neutralizes
the poison he eats.

You're kidding.
Do you know how much
he drinks. I'm so tired
I've been thinking
of declaring bankruptcy.

Gall bladder pleads
they will blame me.
And the next thing
you know
they'll take a knife to me.

Liver sighs.
Okay, Gally, I'll keep trying
and if your extra bile
doesn't work,
I'll send up a little jaundice.

Between the two of us,
your bile and my jaundice
maybe he'll get the picture
and we'll be good
for a few more years.

Toilet Tissue Issues II

One ply, two ply,
five hundred sheets,
one thousand.
Recycled, pristine.
Scratchy, soft.
Fold, crumple.
Flush twice
with new water saver
commode.
Flush once, and dare
the dire disaster
of commode clog.
Please,
Regulate.
Legislate.
Translate.
For the benefit
of all.

What Every Girl Wants

Every little girl,
when she sees one,
wants a penis.

How come you're so fancy
down there,
and I'm so plain.

And that's the start of it.
He swings it around,
shows her
how he can pee
circles around her.

And that's the end of it.
What we get
is a big swinging dick.

Weigh-In

My weight, it weighs
heavily on me,
in my mind,
and on my body.
I think of how much
I weigh, and then
I think of my diet, which brings me to
food, and all the delicious ways
I got fat, and then I feel
a fast coming on, a severe case
of starvation, and so I save
my life with a small
piece of cake, and then
a few more, just to ensure
survival.

The Cross Dressing Cantaloupe

Cantaloupe
likes to fool the crowd,
wears a mask
and feet
dressed up in ballet slippers.

At night,
when the lights are dim
it does the hula,
and sometimes, even

a teasing strip
in which
it peels off skin
and bares its coral flesh.

It even invites a few
to come and take a taste,
but none do dare
except for carrot
who takes an occasional
lick.

As the sun comes up
cantaloupe covers itself
and hopes it looks
good enough
to eat.

Family

A Bedtime Story From a Grandmother

Rebecca says,
Tell me a story, Stessy.
This time a very long story
and a very scary story
about a big monster
that comes down the street
and scares all the kids.

Rebecca says,
Only it turns out all right.
He's really a good guy
and the kids are not
scared anymore.

Rebecca says,
It has to be
a very long story,
and at the end
I have to close my eyes,
and when I open them,
it has to be morning.

Body Jumping

When my mother died
she jumped right in
to one of my daughters.
When she speaks
I hear my mother,
bossy, opinionated,
stubborn.

On the other hand,
my other daughter
is just like me.
When she speaks,
I hear myself,
bossy, opinionated
stubborn.

A Chair for My Mother

Mother, I would build a chair for you,
short enough
so that your feet touch the ground,
with the full and regal back
of a throne.

You sit, clad in one of your regal
self-made designer gowns.

Your mother and father visit you,
love you, commend you, kiss you.
Your sisters and brothers come
to tell you how proud they
are to be your sibs.

And you grow, so full of love,
you need a taller chair.

For Charles

For you, a valentine of
fights,
silences, passion,
children, grandchildren,
gardens,
mourning, jubilation,
dejection, losing, winning,
rheumatism, determination,
high blood-pressure,
low blood-pressure,
temper, calm,
joy and sorrow.
I send you forty years
of my love.

Child of My Child

A miracle, umbilicus
tight around your neck.
Born howling, howling baby.
Dour toddler, sweet child,
Joyless sweet child.
Aidan, have the joy
that Sarah never knew.

Forecast

My great grandmother, who was blind
insisted, begged, and pleaded.
Finally, her grandchild
who was to be my mother
was allowed to lead her
to the visiting gypsy

who took her hand, turned it over, and softly said
Don't be afraid. Your children will always see.

My great grandmother smiled, sat back in her chair, said thank you and asked for more.

Are you sure? The gypsy asked.

Yes, yes, that's all that worries me.

You will live long, but in the end you will be alone. There is a long voyage, but not for you. Your grandchildren will leave you for a new place. They will have children who will never know you.

Never, my great grandmother said. They told me you were a faker, and you are. My children will never leave me. My children and my grand children live with me. Take me home, she said to her eldest grandchild. Your grandfather was right. She is a faker, except for the part about seeing. Take me home.

It came to pass.
We who never knew her,
heard stories about
Our beloved great grandmother
who was blind and
supported her family
knitting stockings
for the village.

Grandfather

It is 1895 and I see you at Ellis Island
after the long walk across two countries.
After the long boat trip,
starving and shivering in steerage.

I see your wife and babies pass inspection.
I see them put a large chalk mark
on the back of your coat.
I see you hide in a corner,
turn it inside out.
I watch you run to join your family,
and pass through to the Golden Medina.

Blue eyed blonde giant
of few words,
now I know you,
and I thank you.

Hits and Misses

I miss my children,
those little ones
who used to think
I knew
all the answers
to their questions.

Now, all grown, and
all knowing,
they kindly answer,
direct, and advise,
even if I don't
pose a question.

I Used To Love

The father.
who didn't love me.

The mother
who couldn't show love.

My sisters, who each
outshone me.

And, do you know what?
I still do.

The Late Late Show

My private movie screen turns on
At two a.m. sharp,
and there, on the ceiling,
in living color,
in full scale
and infinite detail I watch
the replay of my deficiencies,
mistakes of commission,
and worse,
errors of omission.

Watching, I wonder
how those children of mine
grew up, fairly sane
fairly healthy
and of all impossibilities
are loving parents,
and loving children.

The Moon

My father told me,
liked to tell me
over and over
and liked to tell
everyone who
would listen.

As a baby, I stood
in my crib
and kept hollering
for the moon.

Give me the moon
I yelled.
Give me the moon.

When I didn't get it
I threw myself
down in my crib
and cried,
with rage unchecked,
until I fell asleep
with little clenched fists.

Mother Love

My children really love me.
I know they do.
When I visit, and it's time
for me to go home,
they wheel my suitcase,
fearing I will trip.
They walk me to the ticket counter
to assure themselves
I really have a ticket to the correct destination,
and I have a good seat,
and the plane is really going to take off,
and do not wave me off
until they see me going through security.
When they visit
they take over the kitchen,
shove me out of the room,
with a glass of wine,
compliment me
on the things
I chopped and diced and sautéed and fried and baked and broiled
before they arrived.
They hustle and bustle
while I relax,
as they told me,
on a chair upholstered with pins and needles.
How can I tell them
I wish they would love me a little less.

My Father Taught Me

Fun, laughter and parties,
loyalty to family
and friends.

My father taught me immorality,
the lie of truth,
and the self above all.

My father taught me generosity,
solitaire
and gamesmanship,

Above all,
my father taught me
survival.

My Mother Never Taught Me

That she loved me.
That she thought I was smart.
That she thought I was good looking.

It was a puzzle
I had to piece together,
each tiny piece, until

finally I saw the picture
long after it was too late
for me to demand her kisses.

One piece was in the cellar,
in the box of my school papers
which she saved. Only mine.

Another was in the way
she schooled me,
to a rabbi to read Yiddish,

to a Hebrew school
to prepare for bat mitzvah,
which came fifty years later,

to the shoe store man
to whom she whispered
about my regal good looks.

What she did teach me
was to hug and kiss
my children

to affirm their beauty
and their intellect
every chance I got.

Of Late I Dream Correctively

My dead friends come to life
live long and healthy
until they are very old
and die quick and painless ends.

My mother and father
love each other
and stay together
living happily every after.

My kids all love one another
and love one another's spouses
and love one another's children.

My friends all like each other
all like me all the time
and never an unkind word
is said or thought.

Then, and only then,
I wake up.

Photography Lesson

My father breaks my heart,
just by being so young and handsome.

There he stands, next to his wife,
my mother, her mother and father,
her sisters and brothers,
wives and husbands.

There he stands, tall, jaunty,
a handkerchief in his breast pocket,
looking as if tomorrow
need never come.

There he stands, devil in his eyes.
I understand how my mother
fell head over heels,
in spite of no future, no trade, no money.

Oh, Daddy, what I would give
to go back to being
a little girl, and know
how to look at you.

Rachel at Almost Seven

Seven, Rachel will be,
and needs my attention
with a touch of eye shadow
blush and lip-gloss.
She demands party shoes
with heels, sheer tights
and dresses that whirl
as she spins.

She plays the piano,
sometimes with two hands,
and has chosen drums
as her second instrument.
She learned to read in order
to earn a canopy bed,
in spite of her best intentions
to be read to forever.

She gave her hair,
a braid to the waist
To Locks of Love
and is growing it again
for another child.

Rachel calls her brothers
The Boys, and is only
a slight pain to them
as she teases, cajoles
and charms.

Silence

Noisy children
annoy me, amuse me.
A sudden blast of quiet
is the signal they are
up to no good,
working in cahoots
and I come running.

My bed-partner's
stentorian snores
disturb my sleep,
cause grouchiness.
When they stop
I awake to the
drum-beat of my heart.

A Telephone Call

My mother-in-law,
whose name, by the way
was Lena, Lena the almost blind,
the almost forgotten,
buried now,
next to the master of the universe.

One day, shortly after the marriage,
that mother-in-law rang me up.
My son, she told me,
he was always a good boy.

Yes, I said,
I'm sure he was.

He gave me his dry-cleaner delivery money,
so I could buy slip covers.
He polished my chandelier,
he grated my horseradish.

Yes, I said.
He was a good boy.

But if ever, she said,
Please G-d, no.
If ever, tut tu kin ein hura,
if ever, he does, please G-d no.
The wrong thing,
call me,
I'll take care.

Time Warp

I want it to be the time
when I pet my dog,
find Finky, the dead cat,
torturing Tommy, the dead dog.

I want it to be the time
my mother told me about.
The best years of my life,

When I bathed my children,
put them to bed and didn't worry
about where they were,
and prayed for their safety.

When my young husband comes home,
triumphant, tired, kisses me
hungry for dinner, hungry for me.

I want it to be the time
my mother and I
sit in the kitchen
and enjoy a cup of coffee.

Valentine's Day 2002

I awoke with
a bundle of boys
on each side of me
kissing, whispering,
happy Valentine's, Stess.
Two dewy drowsy cherubs,
imps, stampers,
stompers, loves,
seven and five.
My husband, my lover
came stamping, stomping,
put a huge heart of chocolate
on my bed and
a cup of coffee in my hand.
Enough love to fill
the room, the house,
and maybe, the world.

Yearly Visitation

And when the children come
we are happy.
And when their children come
we are very happy.
And when their dogs come
we make believe
we are very very happy.

And when the pots boil,
we are thrilled.
And when the grill fires up
we are very thrilled.
And when we put another leaf in the table
we are very very thrilled.

And when the dogs pee on the carpet
we are not happy.
And when the kids spend
a million dollars every day in the market
we are not thrilled.
And when the grandchildren
liberate our diary and old letters
we are neither happy nor thrilled.

And when the children leave
we are happy.
And when their children leave
we are very happy.
And when their dogs leave
we are very very happy.

Nature

Bigoted Nature Lover

I love birds,
so I feed them.
Not really.
I only like them a little
and I am a bigot.
I like cardinals (the males),
and bluebirds, finches,
better than sparrows
and grackles and mourning doves.
And I like all birds
better than squirrels.
So my bird feeder
shocks squirrels.
Don't worry.
It's just enough
to make them jump off,
and tell each other
to beware.
Once in a while
they send an innocent to see
if the battery is still working.
Depending on the result,
they all jump on
empty the feeder in a trice,
until we replace the battery.
Am I still a nature lover
if I am a squirrel hater?

Don't Say One Bad Word

about winter.
The colder it was,
the stormier,
the darker,
the icier;

It taught us
the miracle
of Daffodils,
Forsythia,
and even
Poison Ivy.

Every Autumn

This is the best one
I say every autumn.
as I walk through
an improbable oil painting,
colors of which
I have never seen
in a museum.

Every day a different
tree or shrub puts
on a show for me.
A few days later
bare branches wave
good-bye.

Hummingbird

The very next morning
outside the window
I saw a humming bird
at the feeder.

Her head was royal purple,
her body a shiny green.
There was no sugar water
in the feeder, but she flew
around, perched, looked at me
until I understood.

Soar, sister, fly, swoop, drink nectar
love flowers, love life, build
nests, speak to me, speak to me.

I Know Rivers

I watch them flow
lush with life,
ferocious.
Children own them.

The river runs red-hot, unstoppable.
Young men and women
Give each other
momentary relief.

Time passes.
The river flows calm
allowing pleasant cruises
on its gentle stream.

Later, rocks appear.
It takes a strong navigator
to bring
the boat ashore.

Water turns to sludge.
Alligators lift their heads.
Currents cross each other.
Only the shore is safe.

Misbegotten

Poor month of March,
truly ugly duckling
of the year.
Winter's snows have turned
to dirty slush.
Empty nests have shredded,
no longer decorate
the highest branches.
Brutal winds make kites of us.
March does its work in secret.
sap rising, buds forming.
Never mind, I love March
for its silent promise.

The Morning Is Awash With Angels

At night devilkin
taunt me with
what might have been
what might yet be.

In the morning
I open my door,
hold tight.
Millions of angels dance.
They make a circle,
beckon me.

I almost join them
until I remember
To hold tight
as they ascend
with the morning
sunrise.

My Field of Flowers

Visits in May for ten wild days.
I walk the path of riotous colors,
every azalea abloom in outrageous audacity.
Yellow, orange, red, white, purple
and every shade in between,
wildly clash, make love to one another.

Tiger lilies and hostas
beg for attention.
Rhododendrons stand tall,
show buds, their edges
rimmed in color.

By July, it is all a dream.
I walk the path of quiet green.

Procreation

I stand at the pond,
the Duck Pond, to be exact
which Canada Geese
visit and breed each spring,
or try to breed, to be exact.

Years ago I would wake
to the loud honks of triumph.
throw on my bathrobe,
walk down the path
to see tiny yellow balls of fluff
on parade behind their proud mother.

These days, someone rows
to the island in the middle
of the pond,
where the mother sits
nursing her eggs.
she flutters up, hovers close
at the intruder's approach.

The intruder greases the eggs,
rows away
and the mother settles down
settles down to nurse
her murdered eggs.

Who wants the mess,
the filth those ever multiplying
geese make.

I do.

Sandy

The opera wasn't cancelled.
The shows went on.
People went shopping
we had no heat, no
electricity.
Tiffany hosted a gala.

My girlfriend had a cancer removed.
Another friend had exquisite pain.
And Con Edison just kept rolling
just kept rolling along.

Is this how the
victims of tsunamis and tornados
and earthquakes feel?
Here we go again,
back to normal.
Except for a few
in Staten Island,
in Queens, at the shore.

I really must remember
to order
my Thanksgiving turkey.

To Spring

You think I'm going to write
something nice about spring.
What's so good about it?
With all the flowers blooming
and me with my nose full of pollen,
sneezing and wheezing.
My eyes can hardly open enough
to see any flowers,
much less to admire them.

And weather,
whether its hot or cold
or nice and sunny
or rainy and cold.
I leave with a coat
and an umbrella,
and I swelter,
or I go out with a sweater
and I freeze.

So what's so good about it?

Life

The Chinese Summer

I swam to China.
Yes. Really.
I swam to China.
At least,
the Pacific.
Each morning
I dared
the heat, the cold
the rain, and I dared
the chilly pool.
I swam and
I counted to
one hundred.
One hundred
back and forths
for four months
must be China.
At least,
Brooklyn.

The New Year

Now that it's a new year,
and I have survived illness
depression, repression
and frustration,
I shall allow only pleasures,
new friends, old friends,
new clothes, old socks.
I shall become deaf
to any disagreeable thing,
blind to ugliness.

All this, I promise,
next year.

Good Old Friend

When I see my good old friend
twenty years later
we are both good and old.

"How are you," I'll say.
"How have you been," I'll ask.
"Fine and fine," she'll answer.
"And you?"
"Splendid. Perfect." I'll say.

Then we will look at each other.
We will laugh the earthy laugh
we shared so many years ago
when it was too dangerous to cry.

Failing Jewelry

We spent a week
at a tropical hotel.
The couple in the next cabin
were very nice, and also very fancy.
The lady wore diamonds to sun by the pool,
everyday a different combination,
all of which were large and beautiful.

We had fun, swimming
dining and dancing.
until one night,
we came back to our cabin,
to find all my beautiful
jewelry tossed on the lawn.
My husband roared.

Your stuff didn't make the cut.
They thought you were
the Diamond Lil next door.
I gathered my chains,
my bracelets, my pearls.
Never mind, I whispered.
I think you're beautiful.

Feast of the Cafeteria

I enter the line
tray in hand.
Waiting for me is
the best mother.

Dear, she says,
a little juice?
May I give you cereal?
Hot is ready,
and here is cold.

My darling,
let me tempt you
with pancakes, French toast,
a muffin, a bagel, a roll,
rye bread, white, whole wheat.

Have some coffee, tea,
hot chocolate, a glass of milk
yellow with cream,
pristine blue.

No, no my sweet.
It was my pleasure.
No pots, no dishes.
Just leave them here
on your way out,
and have a great day.

I Am Moving Out of Grief Street

Enough caterwauling.
I pack my suitcase, open the front door.
Not a chance. It's a one-way street
leading straight back to me.

I go to the back, try to open the portal.
It opens a tiny wedge, and stops me with thorny shrubs.
I arm myself with a poultry shears,
cut away enough to get to the shed, with a machete.

My legs and arms are full of scratches
as I work, the bushes grow right back and laugh at me.
I work harder, and faster, hack a small path,
see what the shrubs conceal.

There is flowering meadow just beyond.
I drop my suitcase.
Who needs a bagful of woe.
By the time I get there the sun is sinking.

I rest under the shade of a large elm.
I hum a small tune.
I cannot remember what it was
that I grieved so long and lie down.

In the morning I will find my way.

I'd Like to Kick the Glitter

out of some people,
and let the truth shine through.

Joe leaves his very tired wife
while she nurses their dying child,
for a younger laughing woman.

Louise kisses and hugs her husband
before he trudges off to work two jobs
and shortly after, welcomes her lover to bed.

Jane and Jerry, members of the country club,
who pay tremendous dues on time,
but short the dry cleaner and plumber.

Margaret, the picture of devotion
who leaves her two year old alone,
just for a few minutes or so.

And as for me,
everyone knows,
I am pretty near perfect.

Instructions for Any Room You Enter

Check buttons.

Stand straight.

Smile as if you know

everyone is waiting for YOU.

If no one is there it's good practice.

If the room is full,

hey, you never know.

It's All a Matter of Taste

As I take a bite of steak
I wonder
how I would taste.

Would I be well aged,
and marbled,
or treated

like mutton,
used for chops
and stew.

Maybe a hen,
and wonderful
for soup.

Yum. Yum.

Ladies and Gentlemen

She asks for the ladies' room.
He asks for the toilet.

She defecates.
He takes a shit.

She burps.
He belches.

She flatulates.
He farts.

She glows.
He sweats.

They hug.
They kiss.

Look at Me

Watch. I stumble forth,
out of the house,
out of the marriage.

Look, I fall, landing soft
into a new life,
learning to walk straight.

Observe. Skipping comes naturally,
to my children and me, holding hands,
learning the joys of the Automat.

Notice the prince in the blue Buick,
who comes driving up, swoops us up
into the rest of our lives.

Observe. We stumble. We rise.
We walk. We skip. We know love.

Love, How the Hours Accumulate

The ones we wasted
in angry silence.
Let us buy them back,
and dance to Harry James.

The ones we wasted
shopping for stuff.
Let us recycle
and play tennis.

The ones we wasted
watching the idiot box.
Let us press rewind
and retire to make love.

Mathematics Must Be True

Every triangle must contain one hundred eighty degrees.
Don't bet your life on it.

There is a thing called Non-Euclidian Geometry,
AND I UNDERSTAND IT.

Draw a line from the equator to the North Pole,
and back to anywhere.

AND IT IS MORE THAN ONE HUNDRED EIGHTY DEGREES
BECAUSE OF THE CURVATURE OF THE EARTH.

So what does that do to the absolute truth of mathematics
which people swear on.

On a Perfect Sunday

We both sleep late,
at least until 7 a.m.

This day,
we break training.
Lox, bagels, hot coffee,
cream, no decaf,
no skim milk.

Still in our nightclothes
we sink into the sofa,
read, do the puzzle,
nestle, and even nuzzle.

It's lunchtime,
and again
we defy
the doctor gods.

Salami sandwiches,
rich with mustard,
and as a token salad,
down sour pickles.

Upstairs for a nap,
which is more than
a nap, happily.

Rising again,
we spend
the rest of the day
watching old movies.

Dinner is more protein,
frankfurters, juicy
with sauerkraut,
our nod to a vegetable.

Another movie,
a few antacids,
and we happily go to bed,
burping all the way.

Terrible Things

When he comes
he brings
terrible things.

The terror
pleasure and
pain

of leather
rubber and
iron.

After,
I must
say

thank you,
as I pay
my trainer.

The Poem of Knowledge

It's wrong to eat anything
that can look me in the eye.
I do.

It's wrong to weigh too much
and eat too much.
I do.

It's wrong to have
a closet full of clothes.
I do.

It's okay to love life.
I do.

It's okay to sing off key.
I do.

Vacuuming Heaven

"That part of my life is over. I pushed a
vacuum for a lot of years, and I aint going
 to push it again until God knows when."

"God does know when. You'll push a vacuum
in heaven. That's just what you'll be doing
on those miles of wall to wall."

"That's your idea of heaven for me?
You think my reward in heaven
is to push a vacuum?"

"Not exactly. You sure will see heaven,
with pushing that upright around.
I got to tell you, for you,
hell is being a cleaning lady in heaven."

What Not

NOT my black toe shoes
which I love to hate because
they were NOT pink, like the other girls had.

NOT the striped taffeta pants my mother sewed for me.
Not the pink tutus the other girls wore.
Was I NOT a little girl, maybe a little clumsy.

NOT my dog, coming to us as Sweetheart,
but renamed Perky, a female,
not to be seen again when her care-giver left.

NOT my dog, Misty, which my husband hated because we bonded.
My pal was NOT to be seen again when I came home from birthing our son,
NOT to be found when I cruised the streets looking for her.

NOT my black bathing suit,
which clung to my nubile frame,
until I realized I was NOT young, NOT nubile.

NOT my babies, now big brawny men and women,
with children of their own, who mourn the fact their children
are NOT babies any more.

NOT my strong handsome husband who
is aggravated when he gets tired more frequently.

NOT me, who walks slower, thinks slower, and
does NOT face the end
with sanguinity.

When History Enters My House

Sometimes the man who built my house
comes to visit me and the house he built.

Sometimes the man who built my house
sits at the piano, and plays a few chords.

Sometimes the man who built my house
walks around, up and down staircases.

The man who built my house
is well pleased. He leaves and the house
is filled with warmth and peace.

For Sale Signs

The houses in our family
all sing aloha, shalom, goodbye.
They sing of love, of babies,
of sickness, of hate.

My mother and father's house
brought joy for one.
A leaden burden for the other,
until the end, a duel,
when the winner lost and
the loser lost.

My sister's houses
didn't last long.
Too much bad medicine,
too much fire water.
They too are gone,
much too soon.

And our house,
the only one still standing
in a neighborhood of teardowns,
we, the only old ones,
hold on tight
for now.

Written in Stone

Stone writing wears
off, wears down.
What was written
Yesterday, the rains
of heaven laugh at.
Forever is a lie.

Age

Testing for Age

A person who
can learn how
to make a
computer go
is not yet too
old to go
water skiing
try skin diving
or
take a new
lover.

Never Mind the Mirror

You are old when
you refer to yourself
as "older,"
hate being called elderly
and the ticket seller
gives you a Senior Discount
without asking.

You are old when
you say
you have enough clothes
to last
the rest of your life.

You are old when
you renew subscriptions
one year at a time.

Life Is a Trade Off

You trade the two a.m. feeding
for the two a.m. bathroom run.

You trade the five a.m. cry from the crib
for the five a.m. snores from your partner.

You trade the eight a.m. school run
for the eight a.m. weary two mile exercise trudge.

You trade the hand chopped twelve noon baby food nourishment
for the twelve noon lunch: no sodium, no fat, and no carbs.

You trade the one p.m. patting baby's bald head for a nap
for the one p.m. decaf tea and a study of you partner's receding hairline.

It takes the five o'clock martini
to make you realize it could be worse.

At Our Age

We should be swimming in shmaltz.
That's chicken fat to you.

Ice cream, twice, maybe three times,
every day.

Steaks, chops, crème brûlée.
Breakfasts of malted milk, and eggs Benedict.

Muumuus, high-tops, or flip-flops.
The scale only to weigh luggage.

Martinis and back rubs,
at least once a day.

Laughing, living, and loving
is our old-age, new age motto.

It's All Relative

For five lying years
I hid my Medicare card
behind my Drivers License.

I came clean, and the
young ones say amazing
when I say seventy.

The old ones pat me,
and say, you're young,
so very young.

A Proper Lady

Look deep inside this old woman,
a devoted mother and grandmother.

Look closer at my socks.
They are what is left of my wild side.

I make myself do brave things,
even though I am afraid a lot.

The mirror is my arch enemy,
when, by mistake I catch a glimpse of yours truly.

I still love fun and parties
and Monopoly and Go Fish.

I know the last roundup is close
but I plan as if I am eternal.

Let death be a surprise.

Socks

Now that I am a woman of a certain age
I have to control my wild side.
Shorts horrify my children.
Too much makeup, they say
makes me look like I am on a day pass.
But no makeup, they assure me,
is a sign I need counseling for
an incipient depression.

There's one thing they can't take away.
It's my socks. The louder the better.
They shout with primary colors.
Colored fish swim on blue cotton.
Tropical birds adorn black ones.
Hearts, flowers, abstract designs
all are secret balls of joy.

Eighty-Year-Old Woman Attends Conference

Alice said
I didn't think you
would be here
this year.
I am so surprised
to see you,
I am glad
you are here.

(You old hag.
Last year,
I thought you
were on
your last legs.
Who could guess
you would last
still another year).

Eighty Four

My happiness is tangible.
I touch it when I touch
my lover, our children,
their babies.

I touch it when I open
my notebook, uncap my pen,
and write something
I do not despise.

I touch it when I pet
my personal tree,
a Magnolia, planted
as a gift, just for me.

I touch it when I feel the
ground under my feet,
and know that I am
still standing.

Enough Already

There was an old woman
who lived in a nursing home.

An old lady, who claimed
to be her daughter
came to see her. It was her sister
trying to mix her up.

Sometimes, her mother came
and held her hand.
No talking.
That was the best.

An old man came.
It was her father.
But he said
he was her son.

She needed
to be with her husband
who left her
all those years ago.

It was too much.
She knew what to do.
And she did it.
No more eating.
No more drinking.

She was going
to be with her husband
who left
all those years ago.

Fifty One Years and Still Counting

I'm married to an old salt
who makes love to me every night.

Some nights he commands PORT.
I turn left, spend the night
with my arms around him.

Others it's STARBOARD,
and he spends eight hours
embracing me.

This old woman
still knows love.

That old man is still
the beloved Captain.

Hotsy Totsy

Hotsy, totsy, that is what I am.
A perfect treasure of smiles
and laughter and bonhomie.

Nothing fazes me, I have no cares.
The glass is always full to overflowing.
Age has not staled my face or body or spirit.

And all around my lovely self,
pigs fly, saluting me,
and singing songs of cheer.

One Hundred Years From Now

One of my great great grandmothers,
I don't remember which side,
my mother's or my father's,
fancied herself a poet.
I think she even wrote a book.

I hear she was a real character,
dyed her hair into her eighties,
lifted weights, went bike riding.
Died on the bicycle.
It must have been an accident.

Senior Marathon

There I am,
running shoes, shorts,
sleeveless polo,
walking, puffing
panting up the hill.

Passed by pony tailed women
on a casual stroll,
who walk and talk,
pass me as if
I were standing still.

One guy
running the other way,
looks at me,
really looks at me,
grins and says,
You Go Girl.
He makes my day.

Visibility Zero

Many women had written about
the veil of invisibility that
drops over a woman of a
certain age. I was ready, and
it helped to know I was part
of a sisterhood.

I was not ready
for the veil to be lifted
so sweetly by so many
well-meaning men and
women, who rush toward
me, to lift my carry-on, to
help me with groceries and
offer their hands for a
steep ascent.

The Old Woman in Two Shoes

I am one millimeter,
one millisecond away
from hag, homeless, haunted.
That cart filled with food
that I push toward my car,
one barely noticeable
seismic shift,
and that cart
contains my life,
and I am pushing it
toward my personal subway vent.

What They Never Told You

1. After menopause, it's not unusual to develop a chronic cough. It is not necessarily a sign of impending terminal illness.

2. Fat deposits leave places where they were appreciated, such as hands and feet, and drift to bellies and behinds.

3. Retirees are not the only ones who go south. All body parts attempt to do the same.

4. It is not possible to eat like a normal human being, and not gain weight. Instead of three meals a day, consider three meals a week.

5. When you smile and laugh, wrinkles don't show.

What Time Is It?

It's never too late for a laugh,
a good belly laugh of a laugh,
a pee in your pants laugh,
a laugh that makes you cry.

It's never too late to enjoy
a bite of chocolate,
a hot cup of tea,
a glass of wine,
a croissant,
a bowl of spaghetti.

It's never too late
to read a good book,
to listen to music,
to write your life,
to paint your life,
to tell your life.

It's never too late
for a hug,
to kiss
your friend
your child
your lover.

Scaladune

I turned myself into a slarrow
so I could dance with hulus.
We smathered up the broadside,
tweeled round the flapso,
shlacked up our tweens,
sayed down, shmuppled and
sontendfed.

Writing

Age Is Only a Number

As a poet,
I am a young thing,
only twenty three.

As a person
I am an old woman,
both wise and foolish.

Foolish to think I can go on forever,
and wise enough to know
how foolish I am.

Eagle

This poem
wants to be an eagle,
magnificent, soaring,
high, high.
But, maybe this poem
will settle for being
a hawk, also big and beautiful,
but not quite an eagle.
Just the way,
I never accepted the presidency.
Scared, that I wouldn't
or couldn't do it right
until I dared
and I did and it was okay.

So this poem won't settle
either.
This poem is an eagle.
A fearsome thing,
reaching unimaginable heights,
feared and revered.

Sometimes a Poem Jumps Out at Me

and won't let go.
It has me in its clutches,
squeezes until every word
is exactly what it wants.

Other times,
it sticks its tongue out at me,
plays hide and seek,
jumps from empty page
to empty page to
other notebooks.

Finally says,
not today.

Writing and Love and Love and Writing

I love to write,
sometimes
and I love what I write,
sometimes.

Writing is an act of love,
sometimes.

I would like it
if I could love
what I write
all the time.

And I would like it
even more
if I could love
all the time.

Yes, We Have No Poems Today

I had a very nice poem,
all laid out in a grid,
spread on the pavement,
ready to go, but
the snow came and
buried it.

The sun came out,
and I hurried to the rescue,
but before I could
reach my poem,
the sun had dried
it away.

I worked by moonlight,
and had a lovely thing
all ready to go, but
the full moon glared
and the stars twinkled
it gone.

So, you see,
there is no poem
today.

God

The Endless War

To start with
we got a pretty fine place.
Flowers and trees full of fruit
and birds and friendly animals.
One mistake, and along
came the evil jokester who gave us
the Tower of Babel,
to make absolutely sure
we would never understand one another,
and in fact, we would hate each other
enough to make the war
that decimates whole populations.
Those of us left watch in horror.
We are punished enough.
Please, now give us peace.
Please peace.
Peace please.

Everything Shall Be Known

The lie wraps itself
in a beautiful golden globe
where it festers, molders
and grows, until
it bursts out
ugly, deformed,
misshapen.

The secret encases itself
in a silver bauble,
whispering, shouting.
until flatulence
cracks the shell,
and the secret,
bare naked
and ashamed
is known to all.

The truth,
poor thing,
has no cover,
no tinsel,
stands alone
tired,
shabby,
victorious.

God, Are You Angry?

Is it because
we are starving, raping, murdering
each other
that you show us your wrath
with record tsunamis, mud slides,
hurricanes, volcanoes, earthquakes.
Is it getting time for another boat?

God, Are You Really An Anti-Semite?

You told us we were the chosen people.
Chosen for what?
Holocausts, ghettos,
inquisitions, expulsions,
pogroms, exclusions.
And now, waiting for
the next incursion
on the "Promised Land."
God, isn't it enough?

God Is Depressed

God's girlfriend asked
what's the matter with you?
You're sitting there, so grouchy.

It's the same old, same old.
Whenever I look down
things are worse.

I've sent plenty of messages,
tsunamis, floods, droughts,
record cold, record heat.

Nothing worked.
I give up, no more looking,
let's go dancing.

God Is Going Crazy

God has a girlfriend
who keeps Him on the straight and narrow.

He's not allowed to interfere
with the stupids who kill each other,

And the maniacs who worship money.
She won't even let Him cure cancer.

It's up to them.
Remember, you gave them brains.

It's not your fault if
they use them for

evil deeds
instead of cures.

God's crazy about her,
but what's going on down there

is driving Him crazier,
and He's seriously considering

crossing them off
as a bad mistake.

Feast on Your Life

There is enough food for the world.
Children die from starvation.

There is enough land for everyone.
People kill for territory.

There is one God with many names.
People slaughter for the name.

With guns, with bombs, with knives,
one inch at a time,

We are turning our Eden into Hell.

I'll Tell You a Secret

I don't believe in God.
Do me a favor.
Please don't tell Him.

Law and Order

People of color
take their voice
and their rage
to the street.

The National Guard
is called out.
The newspapers
speak of riots.
At all costs
quiet is restored.

When my people
were called to the trains,
most went quiet,
resigned
to their death.

Now, critics ask,
How could they?
Where were the protests?
The riots?

How much protest
is too much protest?
How much protest
is too little protest?

Looking at the Moon in Autumn

I feel sad in a thousand ways.
The moon is no longer sacred
or a distant mystery.

We have attacked it,
labeled it,
planted a flag on it.

Who is looking, laughing,
watching mere earthlings
lay claim to the vastness
of their space.

Six Thousand Body Bags

Who makes these things.
Are they stockpiled
somewhere safe
for those
who are not.
Do they run out.
Is there a last year's style.
Are there special sizes
and prices
for children
and babies.

Count Me Out for the Recycle Bin

I died. It was easy. Not like the other messy stuff that went before.
All around me, quiet. No bright lights.
No golden gates. Nothing, until I heard a voice.
Hi. We've been expecting you.

I opened my eyes. Who are you? Where are you?
Call me Joe. I'm right here. I'm not visible.
You're not visible either. Look at yourself.
I looked down. Nothing. I panicked. Where am I? Who am I?

You're in the spirit world. You're all here, but only in spirit.
You can go anywhere, do anything.
You can go to all the places you meant to see in the corporeal world,
You can visit family and friends, dead and live.

The dead ones will be glad to see you.
The live ones will feel as much of your presence as you want.

I have to say that although I had a good life, I am having a swell death.
I've been all over the world I came from, and other worlds I never dreamed of.
I do go to family reunions here once in a while.
I do share jokes with a few old friends.
I have placed good thoughts and good deeds into my great great grandkids.

Let me tell you, it's been a blast.

About the Author

Stephanie Kaplan Cohen lives in Westchester, New York. Her work has appeared on NPR, in numerous literary magazines, university presses, anthologies and newspapers (including the *New York Times*). Stephanie is a proud member of the Authors Guild, and the International Women's Writing Guild. Stephanie is an editor of the *Westchester Review*. Her memoir *In My Mother's House* was published by Woodley. Her poetry book *Additions and Subtractions* was published by Plain View Press and was nominated for a Pushcart prize.

She has held positions as an elementary education teacher, a medical social worker, a teacher/therapist of emotionally disturbed children in the public schools of New York City, a social worker in Family Court, as well as a desk clerk on a Commodity Exchange.

Additionally, Stephanie has enjoyed a life-long commitment to community service. She served as President of the Mental Health Division of Lexington School for the Deaf and as President of Westchester and Putnam County Alzheimer's Association. Stephanie served in numerous other volunteer positions, including vice-president of American Jewish Committee of Westchester and United Jewish Appeal of Westchester.

Charles, of beloved memory, and Stephanie are the parents of three children, three in-law children, and nine grandchildren, all of whom are exceptional in all ways.

www.ingramcontent.com/pod-product-compliance
Lightning Source LLC
Chambersburg PA
CBHW070113080526
44586CB00013B/1284